Crickets and Bullfrogs and Whispers of Thunder

POEMS AND PICTURES BY

HARRY BEHN

Crickets
and
Bullfrogs
and
Whispers
of
Thunder

POEMS SELECTED BY

LEE BENNETT HOPKINS

HBJ

HARCOURT BRACE JOVANOVICH, PUBLISHERS
SAN DIEGO · NEW YORK · LONDON

TO TILLIE S. PINE—
for so *many* things

Special thanks to Alice Behn Goebel for her cooperation,
and to my editor, Anna Bier, for her encouragement and insight.

Designed by Barbara DuPree Knowles

The title of this volume is taken from the poem, "Canticle of Spring."

LIBRARY OF CONGRESS CATALOGING IN PUBLICATION DATA
Behn, Harry.
Crickets and bullfrogs and whispers of thunder.
Includes index.
SUMMARY: A collection of poems with themes of
seasons, holidays, fantasy, and the child's world.
1. Children's poetry, American. [1. American
poetry] I. Hopkins, Lee Bennett. II. Title.
PS3503.E365A6   1984   811'.52   83-18347
ISBN 0-15-220885-2

PRINTED IN THE UNITED STATES OF AMERICA   FIRST EDITION   B C D E

NOV   '84

Contents

"Every bright beautiful wonderful thing."

"I made believe..."

"This hill is mine."

Introduction

The turn of the century was an exciting era in the West. On September 25, 1898, Harry Behn was born in Yavapai County, Arizona, just across from Granite Creek; his childhood years are like a scenario for a Hollywood film.

"I grew up in Prescott, Arizona Territory. It was a wonderfully happy and dangerous life," he once told me.

The Native Americans, who were forced to live on reservations in their wickiups, greatly influenced him. From them he learned about nature—plants and animals, weather and the seasons. He stalked antelope, stirred up quail that whickered and whirred among juniper on lava hills, climbed canyons dark and pungent with pines, and was chief of a "homemade tribe" who called themselves The Mount Vernon Avenue Alley Long Beargrass Tribe, named partly after the alley behind the street where most of the members lived and partly after a Yavapai boy, Charlie Long Beargrass.

Harry Behn often visited Charlie at his camp, sat around the fire, and listened long to Charlie's father telling ancient tales. Nothing meant more to him than the lore he learned as a child from these friends.

In 1922 he graduated from Harvard University. His achievements are many and varied. He founded and directed the Phoenix Little Theater, was an American-Scandinavian Fellow, founded and edited *The Arizona Quarterly*, wrote some scenarios and radio scripts, and founded the University of Arizona Press. He also did a great deal of work in radio broadcasting and taught creative writing at the University of Arizona.

In 1947, at the age of forty-nine, Harry Behn left his native state to live in Connecticut. His first book, *The Little Hill*, was published in 1949. It was a collection of thirty poems written for his three children, Pamela, Prescott, and Peter. Commenting on the book, the renowned children's book critic May Hill Arbuthnot wrote: "The poems . . . range from lighthearted nonsense verse for the youngest to authentic lyric poetry for the oldest children . . . this is a fresh and important contribution to poetry for children."

Other books of verse followed in rapid succession: *All Kinds of Time* (1950), *Windy Morning* (1953), *The House Beyond the Meadow* (1955), *The Wizard in the Well* (1956), and *The Golden Hive* (1966). In addition, he wrote novels, a nonfiction book, *Chrysalis: Concerning Children and Poetry* (1968), and translated two books of Japanese haiku, *Cricket Songs* (1964) and *More Cricket Songs* (1971).

Over three decades after his first book of poems was published, this statement appeared in *Children and Books* by Zena Sutherland, Dianne L. Monson, and May Hill Arbuthnot: "His . . . small books of verse, decorated by the author, speak to young children . . . with lyric charm and unusual variety. . . . Behn's unique contribution is found in those poems where he is helping the child to look at everyday experiences with the eyes of the spirit."

To create *Crickets and Bullfrogs and Whispers of Thunder*, I selected fifty poems from *The Little Hill, Windy Morning, The Wizard in the Well, The Golden Hive*, and *Chrysalis*. The collection is divided into three sections. The first contains some of his finest lyrical images about the seasons and some of the holidays that occur during the year; the second demonstrates his wondrous sense of fantasy; the third shows his gift for looking at the parts of a child's world with an ever fresh, clear eye.

In the opening paragraph of *Chrysalis*, Harry Behn wrote:

My first memory is of a profound and sunny peace, of leaves, birds, animals, changing seasons, spring to sum- mer, summer to fall, fall to winter, and the wonder of being alive. I have tried to capture those early years of primitive awareness in poems and poetic stories. Knowing children better than I do most adults, at least finding their behavior more understandable, I believe them to be a distinct, wise, world-wide dominion worthy of celebration for their cour- age, dignity, and vision.

The poetry of Harry Behn is part of the heritage of childhood; it is my hope that the poems in this anthology will continue to speak to endless generations of children.

Lee Bennett Hopkins
SCARBOROUGH, NEW YORK

"Every bright
beautiful
wonderful thing"

AUTUMN

Summer's flurry
Of green is over,
Apples are ripe,
Mown is clover.

Colors, ablaze
On mountains, burn,
Smolder, and flame
As the seasons turn.

Harvest moon
Comes up at dusk,
Gold as a pumpkin
Or corn in the husk.

But when she floats higher
And shrinks in the night,
Moon gleams with a promise
Cold and white.

INDIAN SUMMER

These are the days when early
   Mists on meadows lift
Slowly into a warm sky
   And silken seeds drift,

These are the sunniest middays,
   The drowsiest afternoons,
The stillest and dreamiest twilights
   With smoky full moons.

Now it is Indian Summer
   When gossamer spiders cast
Their webs among the bare trees
   Where a few leaves cling to the last.

Now the milkweed's fat pods
   Of soft and glossy silk
Crack and curl and open
   Dry of milkweed milk

And the silk puffs up like a pillow
   And every breath you blow
Sends threads of it adrifting
   White and light as snow.

These are the days in autumn
   When gossamer spiders spin
Their webs in a golden stillness
   Before the real snows begin.

THE LAST LEAF

A few leaves stay for a while on the trees
After their color begins to turn,
And no other leaves seem as gold as these
Not even the ones our bonfires burn
With golden flames in piles on the ground.

A few leaves stay so long that I found
The one last leaf on a tree in the snow,
And when a galloping wind came round
The edge of our house and started to blow
Snow dust to sparkles floating free,

When the wind ran away, almost with me,
And sunshine settled quiet and cold,
There, like a bird, still on the tree
Was that lonesome leaf, no longer gold
But curly and brown and dry and old.

HALLOWE'EN

Tonight is the night
When dead leaves fly
Like witches on switches
Across the sky,
When elf and sprite
Flit through the night
On a moony sheen.

Tonight is the night
When leaves make a sound
Like a gnome in his home
Under the ground,
When spooks and trolls
Creep out of holes
Mossy and green.

Tonight is the night
When pumpkins stare
Through sheaves and leaves
Everywhere,
When ghoul and ghost
And goblin host
Dance round their queen.
It's Hallowe'en!

WINTER NIGHT

It is very dark
But not late,
Not after eight.

The only light
Comes from snow
Beginning to show.

Bushes are first
As flakes fall,
Then the top of a wall.

What used to be dark
Is now a hill.
It is very still.

THE FIRST CHRISTMAS EVE

Strange it was
When Kings of old
Left all their ease
And power and gold,
And braved a desert
Waste and wild
To kneel before
A little Child.

Three ancient Kings
Came from afar,
Their open eyes
Upon a star,
A star that shined
On flocks of sheep
Where weary Shepherds
Lay fast asleep.

And when those Shepherds
Awoke to the Word,
Awoke in wonder
At what they heard,
So bright a vision
The star revealed
They could not move
From where they kneeled.

Strange it was
Such different folk
Were those to whom
An Angel spoke,
Spoke of a Child
And filled their eyes
With all the light
Of Paradise.

Strange it was
That men so wise
And men so simple,
With open eyes,
Beheld the darkness
Of the earth
Grow bright because
Of Jesus' birth.

Strange it was,
And long ago,
When Kings and Shepherds
Came to know
The ancient night
And the world of men
Would never be quite
The same again.

WAITING

Dreaming of honeycombs to share
With her small cubs, a mother bear
Sleeps in a snug and snowy lair.

Bees in their drowsy, drifted hive
Sip hoarded honey to survive
Until the flowers come alive.

Sleeping beneath the deep snow
Seeds of honeyed flowers know
When it is time to wake and grow.

MARCH WIND

This sunny wind is only air
Howling in chimneys or anywhere,
So wild and excited it doesn't care.

I let it be what it wants to be,
Shaking leaves awake on a tree,
Rattling branches and pushing me.

But fast as it tries to make me go,
I just turn backward and walk slow
And let it howl and rattle and blow!

CANTICLE OF SPRING

Frogs in the marsh and frogs in the stream
Cheerily chirp in an April dream
Of bursting buds and morning dew.
Wake up, oh wake up, the sky is blue!

Robins are running across the green
Watching to see what is new to be seen,
Watching, listening, down and around
For angleworms hiding underground.

Wake up, oh wake up, a breeze is blowing!
Trillium buds are nodding and showing
Their painted petals as ferns unfold
Out of the moss and matted mold.

Under moist earth seedlings lie
Delving down rootlets, groping for sky.
Look up, listen, touch each holy leaf!
Wake up, oh wake up, spring is so brief!

Deep in a wood, from a patch of snow
Icy tricklings gather and grow
First to a freshet, then to a stream
Over a marsh where buttercups gleam.

Now the singing of phoebe is still,
Now the sun's tide floods a windless hill,
Come where the leaves of a grapevine have made
A tent of cedar, come rest in its shade

And sigh for sweet April so swiftly gone,
Drowse with the bees on a clover lawn,
Listen for stillness, for summer's wonder,
Crickets, and bullfrogs, and whispers of thunder.

SPRING FLOWERS

Tangled over a stone wall grows
A big bush of briar rose.
Its stickers sting my hands like nettles
And its flowers have crinkly petals
And its petals smell as nice
As some sunny kind of spice.

Down beside the river grow
Bluets in a tidy row
Of stars of sky with eyes of gold.
Their stems are grass, and I am told
That they are waterflags, but small.
Sometimes I love them best of all.

But my most favorite flower of Spring
Doesn't look like anything
Except a brown and swampy curl
Of leaf and stem, a twist and twirl
Of rusty green, and you can tell
Where skunkies grow just by their smell.

I do love daisies and daffodils
And scyllas and lilies and roses and squills
And lady-slippers and up in the hills
Bluebells, and bluets down by the rills,
But most I love skunkies. They smell the worst
And aren't very pretty, but they bloom first.

DISCOVERY

In a puddle left from last week's rain,
   A friend of mine whose name is Joe
   Caught a tadpole, and showed me where
   Its froggy legs were beginning to grow.

Then we turned over a musty log,
   With lichens on it in a row,
   And found some fiddleheads of ferns
   Uncoiling out of the moss below.

We hunted around, and saw the first
   Jack-in-the-pulpits beginning to show,
   And even discovered under a rock
   Where spotted salamanders go.

   I learned all this one morning from Joe,
   But how much more there is to know!

MR. POTTS

Nobody knows from whence he came
Or even is certain about his name.
We simply call him Mr. Potts
Who comes and squats on our vacant lots,
   A different one each spring.

We always are happy to see him come
With his red wheelbarrow and green thumb,
His sprinkling can and packet of seeds—
That's all he needs as he hoes the weeds
   With a garden hoe and a hum.

Over our fences, but not too near,
We watch him politely but never peer
As he stretches a string to mark a row
Then slowly slowly begins to sow
   His garden just anywhere!

Nobody stops him, or dares to say
That nobody sows seeds quite that way,
Or stamps them down with a happy dance,
But that is exactly how he plants
  His magic, and wanders away.

Nobody knows when he goes, or where,
But all of a sudden he isn't there,
Only his zinnias and pansies and peas
And tulips and turnips, to grow as they please
  Without the slightest care.

We all enjoy Mr. Potts because he
Is not the old grump he pretends to be,
But a mischievous kind of a garden elf
Who putters about the world by himself,
  Happy, and foolish, and free!

COLORING

A rake, a coat, a meadow, a mill,
A cake, a boat, a house on a hill,
A kite, a spade, and a ball of string,
A wind in the leaves, and the song birds sing—
 It's Spring!
We're outdoors coloring
Every bright beautiful wonderful thing.

Under a lilac bush we've made
A studio with walls of shade,
And in our painting books we spread
Pools of yellow, blue, and red—
　　Carefully,
Though it doesn't matter
Terribly much unless we spatter.

Green and red, and there's a tree
With apples and cherries, and here's a sea
With a wave and a sky and a gull in flight,
And this is the sun splashing light—
　　It's Spring!
We're coloring, and all the birds sing
Of every bright beautiful wonderful thing!

TREE SONG

O summer tree
Singing to me
A song of shadows blue
Spattered with bright
Trembles of light
Leaves above let through,
When I have made
Of sun and shade
A song of summer too,
Then,
O tree
Singing
to me,
I'll sing my song to you.

SUN TIGER

Quietly through the forest pries
The sun into my lazy eyes,
A tiger leaping over trees,
Pouncing playfully to seize
Winds that like scared weasels crawl
Away and hide behind a wall.

When he is tired, this golden cat
Curls up wherever he is at
With a sly, contented smile to doze
And purr and twitch his tail and nose.
His striped pelt is hard to see
In sun and shade beneath a tree.

ENCHANTED SUMMER

Gold as morning, still as sheaves
High on a mountain meadow, sheep
Browse and doze as shadows creep
Down to a glen where wind weaves,
And whispering waters far away
Rippling under silence sway
The morning like a sigh of leaves.

In all the sky no cloud, no wings
Of bird or bee moves anywhere;
Sun hovers high in humming air,

And over miles of stillness rings
The drowsy droning of a bell;
Now, on stone where shadows tell
The hour of noon a lizard clings.

Doves awaken call by call
And quiet echoes them, as light
Folding upon the earth beams bright
On bole and moss to touch a small
And busy beetle, like a spark,
Droning and dancing down the dark
Toward mist of a distant waterfall.

Now the mountains only hold
What light remains across the land;
Up to their peaks in shade they stand
Slowly casting a sheath of gold,
Till only wind is bright where high
Swallows twitter across the sky
As evening wraps the bleating fold.

Out of darkness pours a stream
Of peace, of rustling beauty deep
Over happy hills asleep,
And only one pale glow-worm gleam
In leafy shadow casts a light
Close to dark earth . . . deep is night
In the dreamless sleep of summer's dream.

SUMMER NIGHT

Darkness can be a little too dark
Unless there is *something* to see somewhere.
A cat's green eyes, or else the spark
Of somebody's pipe, or a soft far flare
Of summer lightning across the sky,
Or wings of a gray owl swooping by,
Or a firefly's winking, searching light—
With the least to be seen I love the night.

Stillness can be a little too still
Unless some voice like a sea in a shell
Whispers, or a whippoorwill,
Or I hear the far-off bong of a bell
Across the town, or a barking dog,
Or, under rippling reeds, a frog
Grunting where sparks of stars are stirred—
I love the stillness when something is heard.

"I made believe..."

MAKE BELIEVE

I made believe fly
A bird so blue
It glowed like sky—
   And up it flew!

I made believe grow
A tree in a wood
With petals of snow—
   And there it stood!

I'd love to pretend
A dragon for fun,
Or an ogre—but if
   I saw one I'd run!

So I'll make up a very
Small elf instead
To sing in the moonlight
   Beside my bed.

ENCHANTMENT

In a fall of snow as soft as down
A little child went out from town
   Far and afar away
Through drifting flakes to the top of a hill
Above a world all strange and still
   And lost and far and grey.

And where the child stood on a mound,
Shining upon the snow he found
   A curved and silver horn,
An elfin trumpet on which he blew
One silver note! Away snow flew,
   And lo! 'twas a summer morn!

The sun lay wide and warm and still
Over flowers and grass on the hill
   That glowed with an elfin gleam—
And soft in the valley lowed the herds
And drowsily sang the summer birds
   To a young man lost in dream.

MORNING MAGIC

Sweetly sweetly singing
Early in the morning
A wee sprite brighter
Than a sun beam, whiter
Than a moon beam, lighter
Than a sighing
   Breeze
   Flew
As fairies fly

Sweetly sweetly singing
On bee's wings humming
Underneath a green hill
Trees and trees away
Where everything was—
Till a crow's
   Caws
   Called
Across the sky.

MR. PYME

Once upon a time
Old Mr. Pyme
Lived all alone
Under a stone.

When the rain fell
He rang a bell,
When the sun shined
He laughed and dined

And floated to town
On thistle down,
And what a nice time
Had Mr. Pyme!

ELVES AND GOBLINS

At last I know a very good way
To tell a goblin from an elf!
I was quietly singing a song one day
With no one listening beside myself
When I noticed, bouncing upon a rose
In front of me, a tiny thing
With a peaked cap and pointed toes
Who buzzed, How did I dare to sing
His tune! You see, I never dreamed
That anyone owned any song.
But the way he buzzed at me it seemed
That I was very very wrong,
So I was quiet all day long.

Then just before the sun had set
I saw a cobweb moon in the sky—
I didn't mean to quite forget
And sing that fairy tune, but I
Did sing it softly to myself,
And suddenly bright in the golden air
Appeared what I know now was an elf!

He said how pleased he was I'd care
Enough about his twitter of Spring
To hum it even! Now, when I play,
That wee elf dances while I sing,
And he is happy and funny and gay,
And our laughing chases goblins away.

THE FAIRY AND THE BIRD

When I was small I'm sure I heard
The queen of the fairies speak to a bird.

They perched on a tattered pod of a weed
That rustled because it had gone to seed

And the queen whispered, "It's time to go,"
But the bird ruffled his wings and said, "No."

She tinkled a wand in her tiny hand
And cooed, "Remember that mistiful land

Of marvelous moonful magical ever?"
"I'll never go back," said the bird, "never."

"All summer," he chirped, "I've had such fun
I want to keep doing just what I've done,

Flying with sun on my wings and eating
Beetles and bugs and tweet-tweet-tweeting!"

The fairy sighed, "Then alas, goodbye,"
And touching a thistledown drifting by

She disappeared in a sparkle of dew.
The very next day a cold wind blew.

FAIRIES

What could have frightened them away?
  They weren't in the least afraid of me
  Or a bird or anything I could see,
But softly, Hush! I heard them say,
Hist! and Whist! and Alack-a-day!

Where fairies had danced on a lilac spray
  Blue faded into the blossom's blue.
  I watched them vanish like drops of dew
Soft in a glimmer of misty grey,
But I am sure they never flew.

They simply vanished into air
  As I suppose all fairies do.
  But *why* they did I wish I knew.
Something touched them softly there
And suddenly they weren't anywhere.

Perhaps they heard the distant cry
  Of a wounded bird or a frightened hare;
  Perhaps some creature needing care
Called them away and made them sigh
Alack-a-day! and, alas, Goodbye.

THE GNOME

I saw a gnome
As plain as plain
Sitting on top
Of a weathervane.

He was dressed like a crow
In silky black feathers,
And there he sat watching
All kinds of weathers.

He talked like a crow too,
Caw caw caw,
When he told me exactly
What he saw,

Snow to the north of him
Sun to the south,
And he spoke with a beaky
Kind of a mouth.

But he wasn't a crow,
That was plain as plain
'Cause crows never sit
On a weathervane.

What I saw was simply
A usual gnome
Looking things over
On his way home.

THUNDER DRAGON

A somber dragon,
  Eyes agleam,
A baleful creature
  Out of dream,

Crept over the mountain
  Flashing flame
As down through the darkening
  Sky he came.

Over a cliff
  In coils of cloud,
Through winds that whistled
  Long and loud,

He dropped his scaly
  Carcass down
With a crash of thunder
  Across the town!

No one remembers
  So vast a noise
Since even the oldest
  Men were boys.

No one remembers
  When, if ever,
So wild a deluge
  Roiled the river!

But even a dragon
    Wearies at last,
And so his tempestuous
    Temper passed.

Now, in darkness,
    Away he crawls,
Up to his cave
    In the craggy walls,

Grumbling, growling,
    Back again,
Back he goes
    To his mountain den.

Oh, how his thunders
    Rumble and dim
As he nudges the deep earth
    Over him.

How feebly his lightnings
    Hiss and steam
As he flickers, and fades away
    To a dream.

THUNDERSTORM

The sun looked down at the wide wide land
That was his to shine upon, his to command,
He looked and he looked at the big blue hill
And all he wanted was to look his fill.
He just loved floating in the bright blue sky
Simply looking, but he heaved a sigh
As he watched the big blue ocean below
Weaving sparkles to and fro
Only more brightly than a weaver weaves,
And he watched the bushes building leaves,
And a little brook no wider than your hand
Running bravely through desert sand.

With everyone so busy, the sun up high
Gave a grunt and a chuckle, "Well, who am I
Not to do *my* share?" And that's when he
Filled up a pail with a sparkling sea.
Heavy as it was, he trudged up the hill
Trying his best not to splash or spill.

Not far above went a fat old cloud
With his nose in the air and very very proud
Sailing along without looking, as if
He weren't sailing smack at a steep sharp cliff!
It would have been simple to go around,
But *he* was too important! What the sun found
When he finally climbed up high enough to see
Was that fat old proud cloud snagged on a tree
On the steep sharp cliff, and was he stuck!
Wheezing and bulging and cursing his luck.

The sun sat down on the hill near by
And watched for a while with a smile in his eye.
"It seems you're stuck," he said, "pretty bad."
But the way he said it made the cloud mad.
"I am," puffed the cloud, "and it's thanks to you
For leaving this big blue hill in the view!"
He tried to be proud but it wasn't much use,
He was tired out trying to pry himself loose.

The sun yawned politely. He was tired, too.
He sneezed and said, "I'll tell you what to do,
Tighten up your lightning bolts, give a nudge!"
The cloud gave a heave, and still didn't budge.

The sun sort of chuckled to himself, and there
Sat the two of them glaring, glare for glare.

Along came the wind who was shaking out seeds
From pods of bushes and flowers and weeds.
He saw the sun so he rushed and he twirled
Puffing out seeds all over the world,
Puffing until he was tired to death
So *he* sat down to catch *his* breath.
You know how the wind is, couldn't keep still,
He talked about business the way people will.
"Take dandelions, for instance, what do they care
They have their silly children everywhere,
But when do they ever do a single thing
About them, summer or winter or spring!
They keep on having them even in the fall,
And *I* am the one has to sow them all."

The sun and the cloud both looked away,
So the wind didn't have much else to say
Except, "Very well, then!" He rubbed his cheek
And waited for somebody else to speak.
When nobody did, he went back to work
And shook a big oak tree, gave it such a jerk
He yanked it out of the hill with a crash,
And down came the tree with a smash and a flash
And a boom and a rumble so sudden and loud
It drew, very naturally, quite a crowd.

The crowd was all clouds, they came on the run,
They trampled the wind, they rumpled the sun,

And as clouds do when there's anything exciting
They bumped each other and started fighting,
They used loud language, like *thunder* and *hail*,
And thumped each other with the sun's full pail,
The pail he had lugged up with might and main,
And down came millions of gallons of rain.

The sun tried his best to be dignified
But the clouds got madder the more he tried,
They tumbled hail over thunderhead
Not listening to anything anybody said,
Till the crazy wind grabbed the proud cloud still
Snagged on the cliff of the big blue hill
And tossed him thud on a tangled heap
Of clouds by now piled eighteen deep,
Then he jumped in the middle!

      The last anyone
Could see in the mess was the poor old sun
Worried but smiling, or *trying* to smile,
Way, way down on the bottom of the pile.
And all he had wanted with a kindly sigh
Was simply to float in a bright blue sky.

UNDINE'S GARDEN

I wonder what it might be like
  Under the sea?
I know, said little Undine, sighing
  Wistfully,
I know, I know, because I live
  Under the sea.

When I look up I see no sun,
   My silver sky
Shines back a topsy-turvy world
   In which am I
Till swans like feathery white clouds
   Go floating by,

And then the ripples weave your sun
   Into my sea
In golden webs that sift and sparkle
   Over me
And settle through a waving branch
   Of coral tree.

My colored leaves and vines are bright
   Beyond compare,
Shimmering bubbles grow like flowers
   Everywhere
Drifting unopened as they float
   Up to the air,

And in and out like flying birds
   Little fish
Go nibbling at the swaying vines,
   They dart and swish
Silent in my garden—song
   Is my one wish!

THE WIZARD IN THE WELL

Once a wizard wondrous wise
  Lived in a deep dark well.
His store of lore was more than vast,
  Too vast for words to tell.

No books he read, 'twas much too damp
  Down in his dingy den,
But he was the wisest man in the world,
  The wisest of all men.
So said himself. 'Twas all he said.
  Over and over again.

Thus great renown came to that town,
    Since many a sage and seer
Trampled his beard for many a mile,
Climbed many a mountain, many a stile,
To goggle down that well for a while
    The wizard's words to hear.

And what they heard, all did agree,
    Could never be denied,
So each went home and raised his fee;
Though none was a wizard wise as he,
Proud were they all almost to be,
    And one must pay for pride.

At last the fame of the wizard grew
    Until it reached the King,
And a jolly old king he was who knew
    He never knew a thing.

Said his jolly old Highness, "Dredge me forth
    This wizard out of his well,
Bring him to me that I may learn
    All that he has to tell!"

And so they dredged the wizard up
    Out of his clammy cell.
They dredged him up and let him drip
    In the sun till he was dry.
Then he, of the wonders about him, said,
    "No one is as wise as I."

"No one by half!" the people cried
   And led him, a joyous band,
Up to the King on his royal throne.
The King looked down and gave a moan
To think that such a gnome should own
   The best brain in the land!

But he was kind and friendly and fat,
   He wouldn't harm a flea,
So after the wizard bragged a while
   His jolly old Majesty

Cried out, "Then teach me a thing or two!
   For I am as wondrous dumb
As you are wise. So teach away!"
   And he crinkled a jolly thumb.

The wizard hemmed and hawed and said,
 "This dream that seems to pass
Before your eyes confirms my fears
That nothing is true as it appears
And hasn't been so for a thousand years
 And never will be, alas!"

The King cried, "What!" in great surprise
 And, looking round and round
At the beautiful land that filled his eyes,
 He said, "Not true?" and he frowned.

"It never was," the wizard declared
 Flatly, and that was all.
And a great unhappy silence reigned
 Over the castle hall.

But soon the King began to laugh
 At what he guessed was a joke,
"You mean, of course, and I agree,
The world means nothing at all to me
But what I see, or what you see
 And teach to us simple folk.

"So tell me now, since I know I
 Know nothing about out there,"
And he waved his hand at the far away world,
 "Is it happy and friendly and fair?"
"The world," the wizard said with a sigh,
 "Is dull, bad, blue, and bare."

The King sighed, "What a shame it's dull
  And bare and bad and blue,
But maybe that's how it seems to some
  And wouldn't at all to you,
So why not take a trip outside
  And tell me what *is* true!"

In the wink of an eye, the jolly old fellow
  Was having his whiskers curled,
So off the wizard trudged in a gloom
  To glare at the grim blue world.

He knew quite well what he would find
  About him on either hand,
For he, as he often said, was so wise
He knew in advance what would meet his eyes,
As everything did beneath the skies
  In his travels about the land.

At last he came again to the King.
  "The world," said he, "is bare
And bad and blue and very dull
  And furthermore it's *square!*"

"Ah-ha!" cried the King, "but do go on,
  So wondrous dumb am I
Whatever you say is news to me.
  So the world is bare. But why?"

"It's bare," hissed the wizard, "because I heard,
And I listened closely to every word,
  I heard some ladies declare,
Except for their dresses and hats and shoes,
A hundred of each from which to choose
In a hundred rosy rainbow hues,
  They'd nothing at all to wear."

"A hundred hues!" gasped the King, "You said
The world was blue, and blue isn't red!"
  Replied the wizard, "Quite true,
But, except for roses and robins and brown
Speckles on eggs and a golden crown
On pearly pink castles in every town,
  The world, I insist, is blue."

"Don't tell me it's bad, though?" begged the King.
The wizard looked owly as anything
  As he hooted, "It's worse than bad.

Except for kittens and puppy dogs
And beautiful houses of marble or logs
And a song that everyone sings, even frogs,
　　As if no one were sad,
　　The world is impossibly bad!"

"Then it can't be very dull," smiled the King.
"But it is!" moaned the wizard, "Everything
Except the delicious food and the flowers
And pretty children and ancient towers
And woods and welkins and arbors and bowers
　　And a nice view of the sea,
　　The world is dull as can be."

The King was learning a thing or two,
"All right," he said, "the world is blue
　　Etcetera *but* it is not *square!*"
"Not square!" cried the wizard, "Except for a tune
Everyone sings from noon to noon,
Except for the earth, the sun, the moon
　　And one fat little bear,
The world is entirely, completely square,"
And he showed the King a map, "So there!"

His jolly old Highness crinkled his thumb,
"You're right, of course, but I'm so dumb
The best thing I know is the recess bell."

And he dropped that wise wizard back in his well.

"This hill is mine."

GROWING UP

When I was seven
We went for a picnic
Up to a magic
Foresty place.
I knew there were tigers
Behind every boulder,
Though I didn't meet one
Face to face.

When I was older
We went for a picnic
Up to the very same
Place as before,
And all of the trees
And the rocks were so little
They couldn't hide tigers
Or *me* any more.

SUNRISE AND SUN

Waking into an early world,
   I went out on a hill
And heard no sound, not a whisper of sound,
   It was so still, so still.

It was so still a rooster's crowing
   Misty miles away
Sighed like a sad forgotten song
   Before the break of day.

The stars paled in a paling sky,
   Pigeons cooed, and a slight
Silver shadow of ducks flew by
   In softly whispering flight.

Too early it was to tell a wide
   Wood that was far away
From a little bush close by my side;
   In the grayness all was gray.

But it wasn't long before the sun
   Leaped up and spilled its light
Over the edges of hills, and the town
   And the world came into sight!

Now, nothing at all seems strange to my eyes,
   Or ears, or far away,
With everything its proper size
   In the lovely light of day.

ADVENTURE

There's a place I've dreamed about far away
Where a tropical town crowds down to a bay
Busy with noise on a blowy day.

A warm mysterious coffee smell
Drifts on the air, and a singing bell
Dins and hums on a windy swell.

I've voyaged over the seven seas
In a ship that scuds before a breeze
That sounds almost like leafy trees.

When the morning is wide and windy and warm,
I watch that town from the tall yardarm
Of a poplar tree on my uncle's farm.

THE ERRAND

I rode my pony one summer day
Out to a farm far away
Where not one of the boys I knew
Had ever wandered before to play,

Up to a tank on top of a hill
That drips into a trough a spill
That when my pony drinks it dry
Its trickling takes all day to fill;

On to a windmill a little below
That brings up rusty water slow,
Squeaking and pumping only when
A lazy breeze decides to blow;

Then past a graveyard overgrown
With gourds and grass, where every stone
Leans crookedly against the sun,
Where I had never gone alone.

Down a valley I could see
Far away, one house and one tree
And a flat green pasture out to the sky,
Just as I knew the farm would be!

I was taking a book my father sent
Back to the friendly farmer who lent
It to him, but who wasn't there;
I left it inside, and away I went!

Nothing happened. The sun set,
The moon came slowly up, and yet
When I was home at last, I knew
I'd been on an errand I'd never forget.

THE LITTLE HILL

Windy shadows race
Over a hilly place
I know, a sunny place,
   A secret place.

It's not so far away,
I go there every day,
Every bright windy day
   I go there to play.

Over the garden wall
I climb and jump and fall
Into weeds by the wall,
   And then I crawl

As quiet as can be
Under a hollow tree
Where once a bumble bee
   Bumbled at me.

Then still, so very still
Through shade I go until
I see my little hill
    Sunny and still.

Up through the pleasant sun
Up to the top I run
Higher than everyone
    Under the sun,

High up until I see
Over the tallest tree,
Over town to the sea,
    The blue sea . . .

Here no one ever goes
Because here nothing grows,
Only weeds and wild rose,
    And no one knows

Hidden by woods and vine
Far up in the sun shine
This little hill is mine,
    This hill is mine.

THE KITE

How bright on the blue
Is a kite when it's new!

With a dive and a dip
It snaps its tail

Then soars like a ship
With only a sail

As over tides
Of wind it rides,

Climbs to the crest
Of a gust and pulls,

Then seems to rest
As wind falls.

When string goes slack
You wind it back

And run until
A new breeze blows

And its wings fill
And up it goes!

How bright on the blue
Is a kite when it's new!

But a raggeder thing
You never will see

When it flaps on a string
In the top of a tree.

THE SEA SHELL

When I was very small and lonely
  And barefoot crossing across the weeds
Between our garden and the alley,
  I found a sea shell lost in leaves
And held it close to my ear and listened
  And heard the far-off sound of a sea
The way the sand would hear it, only
  Softer, waving as quietly
As leaves rustling, and there were whispers
  Of children playing along the shore.

The sun stood still above that garden
  Of golden morning, chickens peered
And pecked among the shining pebbles
  And pigeons cooed a lonely word
As sun stood still outside to listen,
  As I stood still inside the shell
Where a sea whispered under an older
  Sky, and a softer daylight fell,
And laughing children who were really
  Nowhere now played games in the wind.

RIVER'S SONG

Here am I where you see me
Strong and brown.
Still, I am far away
Where yesterday I was.

Here am I, shouting
And tossing my feathers.
Still, I am far away
Where I have not yet gone.

I am a drop of dew
Dripping to earth from a leaf.
I am a Sea.

Here am I
Where I was,
Where someday I will be.

THE SEA SHORE

Curves of sand
Change with the tide,
Curves of the clouds
Fall as winds lift
And a flood of sun
Sweeps over the wide
Windless harbor.
Still the vanes shift
To a storm from sea
As breakers ride
Against the shore
And the dunes drift
And sift with a whisper
Lonely and strange
Away from wild rose
Roots and grass.

Curves of sand
Are never the same,
Winds uncoil
In a breathless mass,
Plunging waves
Return whence they came,
For beauty as storm
Or a sea like glass
Trembles in time
Like a whispering flame
Gone as swiftly
As clouds pass
Or grass torn
From dunes, or the change
From blue to green
Of an ebbing tide.

RUINS

Some very nice persons have no use for things
Of wind and rust and dust with wings,
Or dust that broods in the sun and sings,

But I like noons when it's hot and dusty,
And cellars that are damp and musty,
And windmills especially when they're rusty.

I like an orchard gone to seed
In thistles and gourd and tangles of weed,

I like a mossy trough that spills,
And old machinery left on hills,

Deserted barns and earthy smells,
And water shining in old wells.

I like the rumble of a warm
Cloud gathering a thunderstorm,

And gusts of wind that whirl and fall,
And stillness, and a dove's call.

Some very nice persons have no use for things
Of wind and rust and dust with wings,
Or dust that broods in the sun and sings,

But what may seem like ruins of a wall
For me hasn't changed very much at all
From the castle it was, and I hear the call

Of children who lived here long ago
Still beautiful and sunny and slow,
And the secret they know, I seem to know.

LOST

I shall remember chuffs the train
Almost too far away to be heard,
   Chuffing into darkness descending,
   Puffing into a distance unending,
Into a stillness barely stirred.

The train bell sounds across the night,
Deep under stillness sounds the bell,
   A silvery, lonely, faraway ringing
   Over a starry wilderness, bringing
Sounds of a dripping winter well.

No voice was ever more lost or lonely
Than the engine's chuffing call
   Echoing on and on and still
   Puffing farther away until
There is no sound, no sound at all.

OLD GREY GOOSE

Every kind of a barnyard bird
Sometimes speaks a pleasant word
   Except our old grey goose.
All she ever has to say
Is a hiss that means, Keep out of my way,
   For humans I have no use!

Sparrows, of course, and robins and wrens
And chickadees, and especially hens
   Are always happily talking.
Only our old grey goose is rude.
When I ask may I hold just one of her brood
   She hisses and goes on walking.

Her babies would like to be friends with me
But she won't ever allow them to be,
   And rudeness is no excuse,
So I turn my back and quack and crow
To my other barnyard friends, to show
   What I think of that old grey goose!

ROOSTERS AND HENS

Of all the songs that birds sing
My favorite singing of anything
Is the song of a rooster spreading wing
And rustily crowing early in spring.

Or on some morning too hot to play,
The voice of a hen in a scatter of hay
Contentedly scratching, backing away,
And talking soft on a summer day.

Such honest music I love to hear,
Close and dreamy, or far and clear,
A gossipy clucking to keep chicks near,
Or the rackety chanting of chanticleer.

People in cities seldom complain
About popping trucks or a clattering train,
But the music of chickens gives them a pain,
And why it does, they can't seem to explain.

A FRIENDLY MOUSE

The sun was leaning across the ground
When I heard a tiny twittering sound,
And a mouse who didn't seem to be
A bit afraid came close to me.

He sat up and nibbled a leaf of clover
And twinkled his nose and looked me over.
I held out my hand to coax him near.
He washed his whiskers, he washed one ear,

Then suddenly he wasn't there
On the ground in the grass but up in my hair!
I carefully walked into our house
And told my mother I'd caught a mouse.

That's nice dear, she said. Then she saw it was true
And stared like she didn't know what to do
Except to remember that one of her joys
Is to show an interest in what interests boys.

She tried to, but couldn't. She glared at my mouse
And said, *Get that creature out of this house!*
I did. He squeaked a small squeak to say
He understood. Then he ran away.

HANSI

Our dog is not stupid, but stubborn, and so
He simply refuses to notice or know
What anyone else can easily see,
That there's an owl in the tulip tree,
  A big owl blinking its yellow eyes,
  Turning its head, and looking wise.

But Hansi simply refuses to care
To look in a tree to see what's there.
We point and shout and whatever we say
He just turns more the other way.
  It's different, though, when out he goes
  Each morning to read the news with his nose!

CRICKETS

We cannot say that crickets sing
Since all they do is twang a wing.

Especially when the wind is still
They orchestrate a sunlit hill,

And in the evening blue above
They weave the stars and moon with love,

Then peacefully they chirp all night
Remembering delight, delight . . .

TREES

Trees are the kindest things I know,
They do no harm, they simply grow

And spread a shade for sleepy cows,
And gather birds among their boughs.

They give us fruit in leaves above,
And wood to make our houses of,

And leaves to burn on Hallowe'en,
And in the Spring new buds of green.

They are the first when day's begun
To touch the beams of morning sun,

They are the last to hold the light
When evening changes into night,

And when a moon floats on the sky
They hum a drowsy lullaby

Of sleepy children long ago . . .
Trees are the kindest things I know.

THE GOLDEN HIVE

Here you have morning bursting buds
    Of bluebells,
A beetle in green metallic armor,
Swallows darting and dipping, shadows
  Of thunder coiling over hills,
  Raindrops, and sun again,
    And butterflies.

In a golden hive these bees are yours,
    Tracing
Tides of clover down indolent winds,
Dry cicadas ticking and droning,
  Hens dozing in sunny dust,
  All these are yours, your own,
    To remember forever!

THE LAKE

Rippling green and gold and brown
On a silver twilight upside down,
Laurels and beeches and pines awake
A ruffle of eddies along the lake.

Fluttering shadows slowly stir
Birch reflections into fir
As something rustles, a fish, or a frog,
Or a muskrat under a hollow log.

Then, nothing moves, no paw or fin,
No drifting feather's slightest din
Disturbs one planet gleaming bright
And motionless in the lake of night.

THE DREAM

One night I dreamed
I was lost in a cave,
A cave that was empty
And dark and cool,
And down into nothing
I dropped a stone
And it fell like a star
Far and alone,
And a sigh arose
The sigh of a wave
Rippling the heart
Of a sunless pool.

And after a while
In my dream I dreamed
I climbed a sky
That was high and steep
And still as a mountain
Without a cave,
As still as water
Without a wave,
And on that hill
Of the sun it seemed
That all sad sounds
In the world fell asleep.

EVENING

Now the drowsy sun shine
Slides far away

Into the happy morning
Of someone else's day.

INDEX OF TITLES

INDEX OF FIRST LINES

O summer tree   20
Of all the songs that birds sing   70
Once a wizard wondrous wise   44
Once upon a time   30
One night I dreamed   78
Our dog is not stupid, but stubborn, and so   72

Quietly through the forest pries   21

Rippling green and gold and brown   77

Some very nice persons have no use for things   66
Strange it was   8
Summer's flurry   3
Sweetly sweetly singing   29

Tangled over a stone wall grows   14
The sun looked down at the wide wide land   38
The sun was leaning across the ground   71
There's a place I've dreamed about far away   55
These are the days when early   4
This sunny wind is only air   11
Tonight is the night   6
Trees are the kindest things I know,   74

Waking into an early world,   54
We cannot say that crickets sing   73
What could have frightened them away?   33
When I was seven   53
When I was small I'm sure I heard   32
When I was very small and lonely   62
Windy shadows race   58